you said you'd stay

Baylee L. Ehlinger

Copyright © 2021 Baylee Ehlinger

All rights reserved.

ISBN-13: 979-8-5328-3405-7

DEDICATION

This book is dedicated to both of my parents, my three younger siblings, and my beautiful wife. Thank you all for staying.

how to hurt someone:
tell them you will stay
and don't

to feel
can be
paralyzing

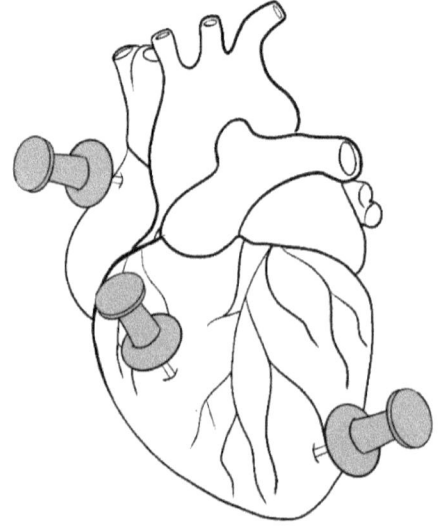

the weather was cold
but so were you

baylee ehlinger

why
is it
always
something

would you have regrets if i wasn't earthside?

i'm such
a sucker
for you

you said you'd stay

maybe after all
this was meant to be

i will long
for every shooting star to ring true
i will long for more
until you return to me

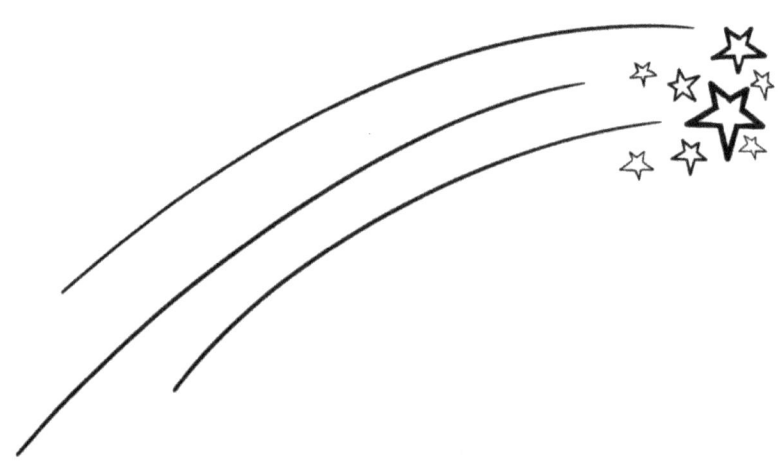

friends come
and they go
and sometimes
only sometimes
they will come back

i asked for peace
but you
you
gave me pieces

coffee gets me through the day
but it used to be
knowing you'd stay

-another lie

the right people
will show up for you
daily

you said you'd stay

oh darling
they won't believe you anyway

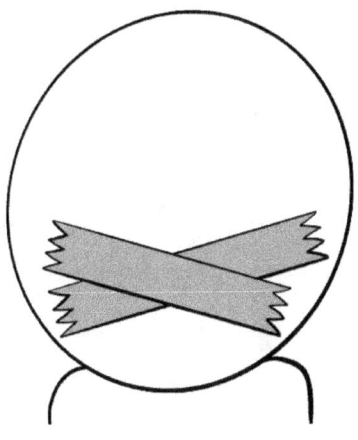

baylee ehlinger

what a fool i've been

you said you'd stay

let me know
when you find the silver lining
tell me
where to look

if it takes a village where is mine?

if i were in your arms
perhaps i'd never
want for more

you left
when things got hard
yet
i'm the weak one

baylee ehlinger

i think it was you
who wore the mask

forever in your world
was not the same
in mine

you said you weren't going anywhere
but
there you went

my nervous system
comes up my throat
with the sound of your name

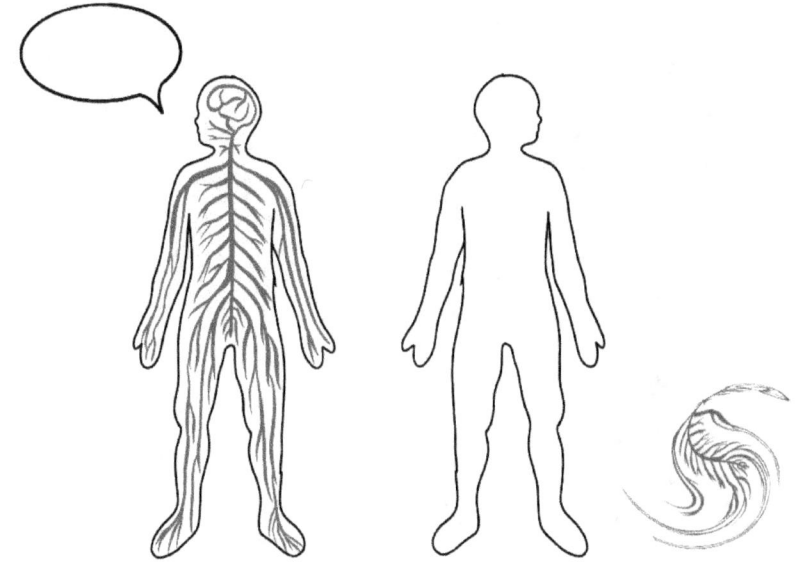

mirror mirror
bring her back

you said you'd stay

i wanted to escape
this world with you

don't come back
i already learned to live without you
and if you come back
i will have to learn
how to do it again
because i know
you never stay long
you will leave me again
you are not strong enough to stay
but it's okay
because
i'm not strong enough to watch you go
again

    -do not come back

you said you'd stay

imagine a perfect world
am i there?

why am i to blame?
because you were there you said

close your eyes
so we can be together
at last

baylee ehlinger

i will drown in thoughts of you

you bought parts of me
that weren't for sale

-thief

i just thought you were different that's all

you said you'd stay

these days are
oh so
long

i've only ever existed in your past

you said you'd stay

when you turn over on your side
to fall asleep
will you reach for my face
in your slumber

is it still called dreaming
if you wake up screaming

your pride was more important
and
i hope it was worth it

baylee ehlinger

no really
i'll be fine
you can go

you said you'd stay

i'll be here
if you return
and
i'll be here
if you don't

you went further than i ever anticipated

you said you'd stay

don't forget the route
you took
on the way back

you left so uninterrupted

i will always have
a welcome mat
for you

baylee ehlinger

we prayed
for different things
didn't we?

you said you'd stay

love does not do
what you have done

baylee ehlinger

it always feels
like winter now

you said you'd stay

it's harsh to call someone evil
oh, but you are

baylee ehlinger

this was a myth
silly me

you said you'd stay

how lovely
says the
unlovable

baylee ehlinger

you are the music
i'm always in the mood for

you said you'd stay

you dealt me a bad hand
but
i thought i'd win anyway

no flower
compares to you

you said you'd stay

why can't you be the strikebreaker

baylee ehlinger

your secrets
were always safe with me

i don't know what to be sorry for
but
i am

baylee ehlinger

you poisoned me
with empty promises
and lies

you said you'd stay
maybe it was
opposite day

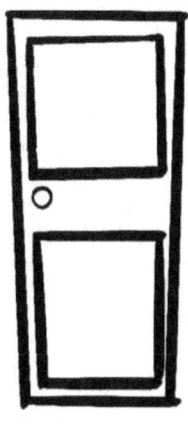

baylee ehlinger

there was nothing luminous about it

you said you'd stay

i don't need your apology
not anymore

you wanted
distance or space
so
is this far enough?

you said you'd stay

will you visit me
in my
daydreams

this is a lesson
i cannot use

like a rose
you are beautiful
and hurtful

baylee ehlinger

i wish time went by this slow when you were here

you said you'd stay

what do i win
for acting
like everything is fine

let me know
when you have a minute to spare

you said you'd stay

i could fall for you
over and
over and
over

baylee ehlinger

your love was flawless
but
your departure was not

you said you'd stay

i ran to you
but
you ran away

i even miss
the way you smelled
like
coffee
thursday nights
magazines
and memories

you said you'd stay

if you wanted to
you would have
but
you didn't

baylee ehlinger

it's sad
what we have become

you couldn't possibly
break my heart
more
than you already have

baylee ehlinger

our souls melted together
but you were
cold as ice

i wanted to fix you
oh
what's wrong
i didn't know i was broken

loving you
was a walk in the park
why wasn't loving me
just as easy

you said you'd stay

i can't cope
with the loss
of you

don't prolong your goodbye
if you're going
then
just go

you said you'd stay

i'd climb
the world's tallest mountain
if it meant
you'd come back

baylee ehlinger

you couldn't give me
a good enough reason
for leaving me
this way

you said you'd stay

there is no
happy ending
sometimes

you said to get rid of the extra weight
is that why *you* left

-i've never felt lighter

you said you'd stay

i practiced in the mirror
what i would say to you
when you returned
but you didn't

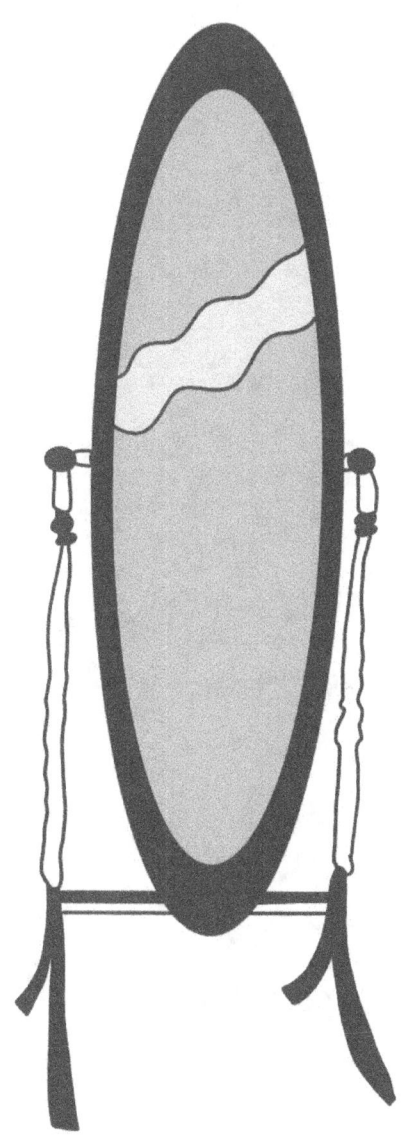

baylee ehlinger

i want to lay on your chest
and hear
every beat of your heart

you said you'd stay

admit that you left
and just stay gone

you look so sad
oh
i feel it
too

transfer me
to a sweeter
and less cruel
place

baylee ehlinger

let me be a guest
at every party
in your town

you said you'd stay

i knocked on the door
but it was a stranger who answered

i want to go back
to a time
when you were
all *mine*

you said you'd stay

i just thought
you'd stay awhile

every 11:11 wish
every shooting star
every prayer
every dandelion
every fallen eyelash
every blown-out birthday candle
every broken wishbone
every penny on the street
was always you

the silence
should've told me something
that words
could not

baylee ehlinger

did it ever occur to you
i don't want to heal
not yet

you said you'd stay

you've stomped
on every last piece
of my heart

baylee ehlinger

when i told you i was a mess
you should've believed me

you said you'd stay

why are ocean sounds
calming to me
but the ocean is not?
perhaps it's like the version
of you
i've created in my head

baylee ehlinger

give me
my secrets back

you said you'd stay

do you remember
when you loved me?
me either

to say what i feel aloud
would be like asking
an impossible but significant question
to which then i just reply *i don't know*
or
i don't say anything at all

i hate
that you can go without
me
yet without
you
i am lost

    -where am i?

baylee ehlinger

you gave me nightmares and called it love

you said you'd stay

my wish has not come true
for if it did
i would have you

think of it like this
i said
imagine our love is a drink
you've spilled it
instead of cleaning it up
instead of a refill
instead of offering me something else
you've left it to dry
you've left

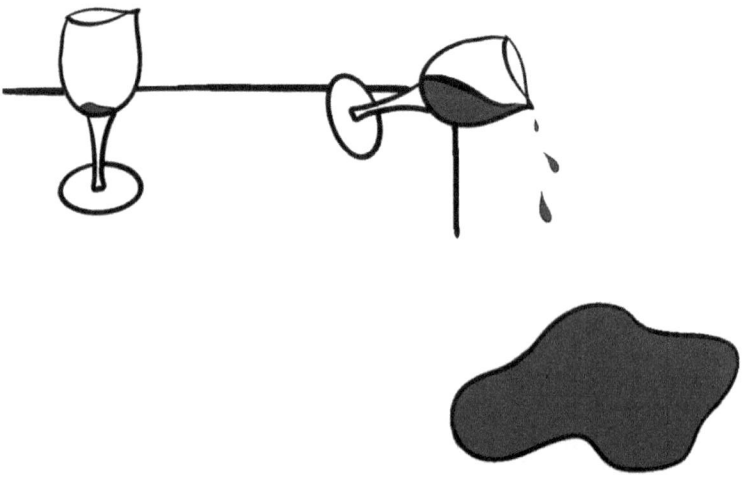

you said you'd stay

i don't exist darling
not anymore

my home
was you
so
where do i live now?

ABOUT THE AUTHOR

Baylee Ehlinger graduated from Texas A&M University of Corpus Christi (TAMUCC) in 2018 with a bachelor's of arts in psychology, and a minor in technical and professional writing. She is a writer, story-teller, artist, and poet. As a graduate student, she wrote and illustrated her first *ever* published book, *you said you'd stay*. Baylee wrote the majority of her poems in this collection while trying to understand life as a 26-year-old with anxiety and depression. The poems within this collection were written with broken relationships, codependency, and loss in mind. Baylee hopes that readers find comfort through this collection as they, too, try to understand the battles of life.

www.ingramcontent.com/pod-product-compliance
Lightning Source LLC
Chambersburg PA
CBHW070421220526
45466CB00004B/1493